STILL

Also by Sandra Meek

An Ecology of Elsewhere
Road Scatter
Biogeography
Burn
Nomadic Foundations
The Circumference of Arrival (chapbook)

Deep Travel: Contemporary American Poets Abroad (editor)

Still *Poems* Sandra Meek

A Karen & Michael Braziller Book
Persea Books / New York

Persea Books, Inc.
90 Broad Street
New York, New York 10004

Library of Congress Cataloging-in-Publication Data

Names: Meek, Sandra, author.
Title: Still : poems / Sandra Meek."
Description: First edition. | New York : Persea Books, [2020] | "A Karen and
Michael Braziller book." | Summary: "In her fierce new collection, poet Sandra Meek
subverts Renaissance still-life painting in order to illuminate the perhaps
irreparable natural and cultural harm inflicted by colonial forces, even those that manage
to create a certain beauty from imperial spoils"—Provided by publisher.
Identifiers: LCCN 2019032304 | ISBN 9780892555055 (paperback ; alk. paper)
Subjects: LCGFT: Poetry.
Classification: LCC PS3613.E372 S75 2020 | DDC 811/.6—dc23
LC record available at https://lccn.loc.gov/2019032304

Book design and composition by Rita Lascaro
Typeset in Perpetua
Manufactured in the United States of America. Printed on acid-free paper.

Contents

3rd Cabinet

4th Cabinet

ACKNOWLEDGMENTS

About Place Journal: "Still Life with Lightning Whelk and Columbarium"

Agni: "Still Life with Zodiac Boat and Glacier Lagoon" as "Still Life with Zodiac Boat"

The Believer: "Still, with I"

Birmingham Poetry Review: "Still, with the Coming Extinction of the Southern African Donkey" (as "Still Life with the Coming Extinction of the Southern African Donkey")

Boston Review (online feature for National Poetry Month): "Still Life with January"

The Chattahoochee Review: "Still Life with Turkey Buzzards (*Cathartes aura*) and *Trametes versicolor* (Turkey Tail Mushrooms)," "Still Life with Wisteria Syndrome and Marula"

Conjunctions (Special Issue: *Earth Elegies*): "Still Life with Caribbean Reef Squid (*Sepioteuthis sepioidea*)"

Denver Quarterly: "Still, with Severed Tongue: *Cymothoa exigua* (Tongue-Eating Isopod) and *Lutjanus guttatus* (Spotted Rose Snapper)"

Letras en Línea: "Still Life with Evolution: Amblyrhynchus cristatus (Marine Iguana), Fernandina, Galápagos" (with Spanish translation by Mary Crow and Francisco Leal)

A Literary Field Guide to Southern Appalachia (University of Georgia Press), edited by Laura-Gray Street and Rose McLarney: "Still Life with Bloodroot (*Sanguinaria canadensis*)"

Nelle: "Still, with Glacier Mouse and Rock 'em Sock 'em Robots"

Terrain.org: "Still Life with Cupped Ear," "Still Life with White," "Still Life with Flag Trees and Bone Chandelier," "Still Life with Damnosa Hereditas and Dark Constellations: USS *Arizona* and Llullaillaco Maiden"

Web Conjunctions: "Still Life with Dysphonia," "Still Life with Cochineal and Zapata's *Last Supper*," "Still Life with Phantom Crane Fly and Vanity Mirror," and "Still, with Trip"

Witness: "Still Life with Scenic Drive: *Strix varia* (Barred Owl), Bikers, and Boar Hunters" as "Still Life with Scenic Drive: *Strix varia georgica* (Southern Barred Owl), Bikers, and Boar Hunters"

Thanks to the editors of these publications; thanks to the Poetry Society of America and judge Mark Wunderlich for naming "Still Life with Bloodroot *(Sanguinaria canadensis)*" as a finalist for the PSA's 2018 Lyric Poetry Award.

Deepest gratitude to Gabriel Fried, the most brilliant and patient editor I know, and to Karen Braziller and Michael Braziller, founders and directors of Persea Books, and to everyone else at Persea who helped make this book happen. Working with Persea has truly been the joy of my literary life.

Thanks to artist Kevin Sloan for letting us use his gorgeous painting *Cache Reef* for the cover, and thanks to José Daniel Guerrero Vela for his guidance in showing me the wonders of the Galápagos, and for his friendship, expertise, and generosity in our long correspondence regarding that most amazing of beings, the Marine Iguana.

Thanks, always, to my sister Linda, my best friend and advocate, for life-long support, for companionship through so much of the travel and stillness which rayed forth this collection, and for being there for me and with me, still, in times of darkness as well as moments of wonder.

Still

A certain angle, itself
uncertain, jewels
a streetlight
as a window's lit wick

to rain-slick skin,
a mushroom's wart-
studded cap sprouting
the median between

traffic, divergence.
There were times
I imagined motion
could save us. O

bloomed bouquet
of mismatched seasons,
O cabinet
of wonders: these

are not those.

Still Life with Dysphonia

In the palace of music, a gathering of the mute:
this became the body.

In the asphalt's cracked path, a clutch
of frog eggs: a teaspoon of froth, a shoal of dark water

haloed blue. Mouths spooked open

to O, the choired sky; double
artifice, the trebled singers spoking the hall's

spectacular skylight: coins of stained glass pooled
to a colossal droplet poising

the milling audience, bronze and copper

and gold. To make matter what wasn't
between you, you said *I*

love you. Imported for this particular

drift, swan that circled the park's tiny island, alto
clef of her neck in reflection among cypress

knees, a child being photographed in her dotted-swiss best

among the groomed daffodils. All those belled
golden throats. Click.

Click. The shuttered air recalling what you cupped
your ear to—the steeled tracks, the disappearing

parallel—what you lowered to the dampened
ground for, what you clear

your throat for: what isn't

coming, though the soldered ceiling wheels
its staff of glazed bones above you:

The baton already lifted, cocked.

FIRST CABINET

Still Life with Cupped Ear

Not flying buttress but fly-
on-the-wall crest, pressed white
as sugar, icing the stone arc

of an interior arch: a shimmer somewhere
between cut diamonds and glitter-polish
on the bride's left-hand nails pale

against the bound stems she clutches
like a girl the May Day bouquet
borne for the granite Leader's great

unveiling. Lieder sung
underwater: *The Meat Queue*, Stalin's fronting
one row Czechs, one Russians, happy

Comrades all. When the Soviets dynamited it
from Letná Hill, some said the head rolled
whole into the Vltava, that great falling

from favor surfacing only
as a fading tracery of widening
circles, like lace shaken

from the drift of swans. Like a salting
of the fields, an arm swing's mimicking
the broadcast of seed, the blown bones' dust

settled the people's shoulders, the Great Overseer dispersed
to a great listening. A word overheard, any grace note's
staccato report, can be played

back as key tone; any echo sustained
made a gathering. Held in the wavering weight
of a single pitch, an hour glass's sand

spilled onto the skin head
of a drum will settle each time to the same
spidery design. Four winds. Four cardinal points,

3 and 6 and 9 and the hands' seal at midnight
indistinguishable from noon: what an A
clocks to, an anthem's operatic close

in the throat raising through sympathetic vibration
the precise flatline the concert master's wasted hand
drew from horsehair dragged across catgut

tuning the orchestra at Terezín. Tracking
the river's skin, the seasonal murmur
of ice crackles to the shatter of heel-

crushed glass wrapped in a bit
of lace, the groom looming
above fragments of the light bulb

which replaced the crystal goblet for its ease
of breakage. Tracking the shatter unearths
that the electrician who served as model for Stalin

drank himself away from that nickname
which ate at him through bar mates' acid back-slaps;
of the worker who chiseled hammer and sickle

into Stalin's jacket button outsized to a swan's
wing span, there is no record.
Like a train so distant it almost

can't be heard, though it drums
the earth, boxcars of names blacken
a synagogue's walls towards the bomb-

sheltered pitch bricked behind the Gates
to Nowhere, concrete bones of a never-
completed museum sprayed with the names

of skaters who air walk the blasted plinth above
where the sculpted blade of a giant metronome
now scythes that swath of air ghosted

with the missing: wheat fields, *The Meat Queue*,
and its artist, all mention redacted
from the unveiling after he followed

his lost wife by cradling his own head
in their apartment's oven, climbing the whisper
of an absent flame—as if once the scales

fell from the eyes there could be
no more music. Just a small
blue hiss.

Still Life with White

After Jean-Baptiste Oudry, *who set the style for the light-filled still life of the Rococo. . . . [and] illustrated his theory in his* Etude d'objets blancs, *a painting . . . that caused a furor at the Salon in 1753.*—*Still Life: A History*

At the MoonPie factory, gravity begins
the line, attic vats of marshmallow batter
a man called Red churns decades
with an oar. White water: the river is deadly

yet too shallow to sound. Oudry on painting
the many gradations of white: One is not
the other. Bone china. The hungered
plate. Ivory napkin balled in the fist

of *peace and quiet*; Sunday dinner's
white-knuckled wake of another
tabled week the son didn't come
forward to be washed white in the blood

of the Lamb. Fathom
as first music heard of the word *you
are a waste*, that melody voiced
from a white fugue of bedroom walls

even before the crib's bars drop down
to what ratchets and mutes but washes
over always as a white-capped
rippling of waves. Breakers. Falls. Rapids

are ranked by air entrained
into water but anyone who's lived
on its skin knows the terror in capsizing
is not being borne by a head

of froth but the veil that held
away the hard body bulked beneath
being rent. White the head of the hymn's
held note. White the sheet that stems

the music. White the furor uncurtained
by Oudry's big reveal, not for his fine-
tuning the hand to temptation but for the white
duck's not being lost to the white wall he'd imagined it

strung against. White without
white-out, blizzard vertigo scrimming sky
to field to a highway's dotted white breakage
blurred to the swim of breathed ice

no one came to break from a white-
masked cow's glazed face. White gown. White
hood. White the hemmed garments of the chosen
to be chosen. Not albinos

but mutants, the white squirrels
of Transylvania County descend from a single
carnival-fled pair, all so puppet-wicked
by genetic memory that alarm still

spread-eagles them against black
oak trunks as the white-hooded raptor
dives down. Rapture catching the congregants
in fire. The boy cold ash. White

shame, white anger, white flag of the spread-
open body. Not the talons of a stranger
but the sizzle at the crossing
of wires. White spark, white ash. White

the saddling weight of sugar sacks unloaded
from boxcars docked to the factory spur's
two taut strings. The Christmas morning
the father caught the son picking out "Amazing

Grace" on the guitar, he took the gift away
for good. Because God's music is only what's held
within His given body. A cavern of sweetly
steeped organs. Glint of his ring making Os

of moonlight, the fretted world clacking away
on its slats. A sheep slaughtered in a country of ice
and volcanoes revives a years-cooled eruption
through the embered sheen of her lungs. Without slicing

open the body, who'd know she'd breathed
her entire life as stone? Little lamb,
how your father must have drawn heart
from the white-listing of deacon after

deacon to continuing visitation upon his child
in the family kept *intact*: tucked-in, tacked
to bed sheets, arms pinned like the veined
cellophane wings of a crane fly stuck

to strokes brushed through oil. In trompe
l'oeil, who can resist putting out a hand
to pick the oily fruit? If *idle hands are the devil's
playground* let us consider the work

of our own. The white duck hanging
from a tag signed with the maker's name
is not the white wall it's been backed
against. Because in the Book of Life

the names are few and composed
not of the born but the born into grace
as immersion, to choose not to be swallowed
is a stain on the white garments of the father's

heavenly dress whereas the surviving
mystery of *The White Duck* is who sliced it
from its frame. Treasures on earth
as in heaven, white loaf that feeds

the many. When MoonPie cookies
are cut, the lace of dough severed from circles
is saved, slung back into the machine, punched
into cutouts of sweetness itself, but crystallized

frame by frame is how the memories return
like the tiny chilled eggs in the Sunday hen
your mother split open to show you
how those shrinking jelly globes trail back

into the body like a reverse stop-action film
of the baseball coming at you
from his hand. White belly twisting
between seams of red thread. Black plugs

of tobacco like pellets taken
into the mouth. Because family is a chain,
when Sunday after Sunday you did not go down,
the anger your father felt was for his own

salvation. That sentence of little Os trailing
to a simulacrum of perspective, a facsimile
of eternity spliced by the body's beginning
and end. The lost history of ice,

compression, moulins' windmills
swiss-cheese with melt the retreating
glacial snout; those jagged bites climbing the ice,
footsteps masked by crampons, little machines

blading the sole with an armored silver lining
forged to a fox trap's frame, to mandible split
from skull, lacquered the thinnest
layer of gleam. Arm both anchor

and axe. Whether the duck was stilled
with a twist of human hands or the preferred
firearm of the time—swerve indelibly stamped
in its finish, the Damascus barrel's coiling

strips of iron and steel permitting shooting
even midflight—is not pictured. If the not-
white thread in the white is what makes white
visible as white, if the father is the machine

of God, the worker of His Own Hands, explain
those nights the mercy of memory reversed
washed clean into white-out
for decades. A cappella, a boy learns to sing by picking

out his father's voice, straining to match what nature's placed
out of his range. White pillar fisted between red
columns of Word, how recover the weeping
salt of the body without winding again in those

dampened sheets? Oudry was famous
as the wizard of whites, but that man heading
the MoonPie line, not whether father or son or the sizzle
at the crossing is what I know but only

into each batter vat as he tipped it towards the final
vanilla sheathing, he spit a single stream
of tobacco juice. Because Father
meant Word, and grace, that ribbon of white

flicking away in the upward flight
of mourning doves pools still
to the hood of an eagle shot to a graveled
shoulder, what *protected* means to the one

who can depend on the light always
to have his back, little lamb, you unpeel
the silvered foil, again you bite
through the bitter vein

slit to beget that exact, exacting
marshmallow white.

Still Life with Flag Trees and Bone Chandelier

Like arrowed feathers posed
to steady flight. Not to become

wind's dolls. Evergreen *there*, backs
                to what wears: absence
absent from this chandelier's full nautilus

spin, chapel of shadows fashioned from the body's

every bone, studded with skulls
wicked to candlelight——moth-flits tongued thin
                as stars when the snows first

creep in.
                Before the needles bottle, witched
to icy picks. An infant's splayed

§

finger-bones.

                What seams the light,
shadows the prayer: here

the sacrum, lateral cuneiform, trapezium: here
                ulna, patella——rather than crystal's
strung charms, the radius ribbed
in octaves. The pelvis's

stilled wings. Plague's revelation, this

§

particular pearl, frill where the jaw
tore away, skull by skull——

                    no singularity,
fusion; beneath the dearest face, that same

stalled swim. World

§

in free fall, any near miss: say a road's

sudden dive, a bike's zag and buck and the child burning
along that graveled shoulder, knee ground

to its ivory cap.
                    Beneath the blood
staunched, the layered flesh graveled

with grit: like a road's bisection, snow banks

seeded with mosquitoes rising from melt
ending the one family picnic one

§

still remembers—

            August was an excavation,
then, tree line a road's coring through weighted

remains. Before the range unghosted
        to mirror the cloudless sky trapped in the lake
at its feet, unchained from any

narrative spine, any lying
on the back telling *that is a castle that*
            a horse galloping that a house

§

going up in smoke—

Electric and cold, what I remember
of white:
         white room, white light. Woman in white
tweezing shatter from my knee; the bone's glacial retreat

as she stitched. The x-ray starred

by the single grain she missed: forty years
its bite a wintered

§

insistence.

      Windthrow, when the roots, not
the spine, no longer
hold: just before alpine, hung by a wire

of wind—then, the gravity of flight. Angels
    of blowback, white limbs

against an emptied sky—

      There, there, she
was saying. *There, there*, white hum
as she sewed, sowing that one

    missed seed—stone
against stone: correspondence,

that small ticking.

Still Life with Scenic Drive: *Strix varia*
(Barred Owl), Bikers, and Boar Hunters

Where ranges meet, the season
unladders: Autumn redacted, Appalachian forests

daggered brown. A corrective,

light; morning, entrails of exhaust—the breath,
missing, restored

as drift, as up-scooped palms of mist, the lake brimming its thin
emerald towers. What didn't fly

the shattering—that blur, what even in the swim
of window glass flashed *animal* through the leaves'

jade and liver-spotted screen.
Poplar, oak. And that purr, mechanical,
driven—

So many curves in so few miles.
The radio-collared dogs too far out to call in.

Unmarkable, the point of entry; exit

woven into view—one branch-tangled wing fanned
beneath the head's dangling; one wind-rifled,

canvassed by sky. The eyes, sealed, light as a saint's
inward turn, prayer the pause before insects

worry their way in. Every curve

cornered, riding north; every bone bulleted green
with flight, ankle skimming the dashed
white line, angling an angel beyond

your place is— steel cages nesting the bed,
the pickup quickened south by that urgent

adrenal hollow, *where are you*, white line crossed over

to smoke the body breathes
this season into air, world now a falling and sometimes

spread wings.

Still, with Severed Tongue: *Cymothoa exigua* (Tongue-Eating Isopod) and *Lutjanus guttatus* (Spotted Rose Snapper)

Did you feel it, that first prick
at your throat, at my arrival's
muscled root, finale to parting
your gill's frilled arc as smoothly

as a hand slips into the silk slit of a girl's
sleeve? How I hummed your heart's
double-chambered thrum, all my jaws
aching me on. Vessel

by vessel, I sawed with a grace
surgical and determined; bathed anew
each gasp, wasn't I wrapped in the blood
of abandon, a sustenance never meant

to sustain? Thus I was eager
for atrophy, the late-stage withering,
your unstrung tongue drifting down
to the fire coral, blades burnt gold

and white-tipped as ash or the needle
eye of flame. There it was set upon
by others no longer my concern—
their dawn-rose blush, gold ellipses

stippling the silvered scallops
of their scales—I, wanting nothing
but to ride your liquid pitch as you troll
the mounded, opalescent ledge for what darts

from its kinks and dark crevices,
when I latched your sweet stub
for good, why, at that dearest jointing,
did you O your mouth, though nothing

swam near to feed us? Only that slow
undulation twisting above coral all mouth
and anus and sting, extended tentacles fine
as a boy's faintest chin hairs. If you

are host, am not I the master-mistress
of ceremonies, oracle to your priest?
Am not I poles from my brethren
who ride their lives out on the surface

of a face, never getting beneath
the skin, the scales? Benign.
Symbiotic. Meaning, too timid
to cut in. Poles from my land-

stranded cousin, pillbug that fear
helmets to a ball small as the eraser
of the pencil any grubby child
might poke it with. Hyphen

and hinge to your hunger
satisfied, didn't I heal the wound
I cleaved you to? Still, you would dream it
blooded and pulsing, eel-sleek,

branched high in the staghorn
ululating the duration. But isn't dullness
a kind of relief, living as the flipside
of serration? And don't I have dominion

over the fish of the sea,
banishing even your burgeoning
phantom limb from this vaulted chapel
I lie in? Because you did not take

the bait descending from sky hung
on a wire dyed the exact cerulean
of the shallows that held you
through aftermath, what came

came from sea itself,
from the very waters that rocked
you, from which you could not
at once have sealed yourself safe

and breathed. All your life now
I will be the live thing ghosting you
from inside, the slick of my eyes
last vision for prey or for kind,

whomever you open your mouth to
as if you might speak.

Second Cabinet

Still, with Glacier Mouse and Rock 'em Sock 'em Robots

                    My palm the measure
            of your weight, stroking you, Pet, we
                    were never rodent, though others

named us so. My Moss-Darkened Stone,
            my Precarious Pebble balanced
    on a pinnacle of ice preserved by your own
            small shadow, all but its spindled core

nibbled away—how your head teetered
    on that long blue neck, that narrowing
            spine: you, Tiny Crow's Nest screwed
                    to my mantle's bottled ship tweezered
            to fascinate; your mast's steeple eaten
                    to a crystal needle, what course left

but fall? Rolling your bare back
            to sky—creeping over you fully
    my green fur, my emerald glove, wasn't I there to soften

the blow, to catch you, always: my garden-level room on your way
            to school, my stock of toys sucking you
    in; didn't I play well your Red Rocker in that plastic
                    arena, letting you strike my Blue Bomber
            again and again, popping my head off

at the root? How is it strangle, how
            choke, to cultivate a green world no one else
    would grant you? You, grown now and scoured
            clean, have you forgotten the springtails,
                    the water bears I hummed

alive in your new skin? Remember I taught you
    they could not be killed—not by boil, not
      by freeze, not by the near
   absolute zero-total vacuum-cosmic radiation of being fired

into space. Remember our desiccation
    happened only when you were taken
  from the ice, the moulin's trickle swelling
     to roar, the glacier swiss-cheesed with melt
    like seams of maggots in venison strung
     to rafter-dry to the jerky I
treated you with, the too thickly cut gift others

would deny you. Without me, what were you but a bit
  of grit on ice? A tiny decapitation memory recovers
     as snow globe, sparks gravity swirls to a blanket
    of glittering ash— Tell me, what world isn't
  made of fracture? So what if the sky's falling
     as a splintered mirror you'd puzzle

your own lost face by? In shatter, recall
  that diamond-dust air, that weather
    that whelms you, that with a flick of my wrist
  I birthed it, so easy the labor
    by which into this bright

I bore you.

Still Life with Turkey Buzzards (*Cathartes aura*) and Turkey Tail Mushrooms (*Trametes versicolor*)

What ruffles the eye, leavens the wound:
the downed oak's weather these snail hooves flare

into fans—arcs of ivory parchment, fawn, indigo ink—banded
more agate than rain. To gather

is to disappear, is to corkscrew
to an unstalked ellipsis the sky

serrated a lashed blue eye by that extension
of wings as what's plucked parches

to weightlessness; what zeroes the gyre
grounds to a clearing, asphalt and smoke a doe

materializes to, dry-iced by morning, river's
bend. Legs snapped at the dotted white line

triggering descent. To *figure* is to fix
the eye to one particular rosette

rising from rot; to *vehicle* is to tenor
the circling, halving the flight

unfurling; is to render one smoke, one meat
tendered at the intersection of pine woods

and tarmac, a human face blossoming
at the wheel.

Still Life with Cochineal and Zapata's *Last Supper*

To harvest color, lobe by lobe the cactus is shaved
clean of its colonies—each gravid insect

a fugitive cargo of eggs carmine-steeped, encased
in ash: like a gray sweater pilling, then the bright

starburst in the palm. The open-limbed view the ring of disciples
unhinges to: *cuy*, enduring indigenous meat—splayed

on its platter. The crimson cloak. The pale wafer
of Christ's face: the better half of betrayal, like virga hovering

above fields of prickly pear, all those
atmospheric optics—sun pillars, hole-punch clouds, a sunset's

claret. Fall streaks. And the dry
equation of scripture: his left hand clutching a small

pillow of bread, two fingers of the right tensed toward his own
glowing face. Bread, body. Like rain that ignites

the fire, never grounding—the sky torn, the bolt
descending: *One per version of the sacred* is one

definition of *savior*; *to rescue*, to gather the clipped
to *sanctuary*: vicuña, sheared of her stellar

virgin wool; puma, claw-plucked to prowl a discotheque's
thumping floors. A condor cropped

to a farm of feathers. The city's station: to quarter
the quartering, each limb freed from the resisting

body; to frame the church-studded plaza hung
with oils. Zapata's *Supper*, absent the lamb, a seamless

jointing—what measure subversion, what measure
struck faith? At the heart of the sanctuary

at the heart of the cathedral riveted from the old city walls
gnawed to their crux, to an unserifed sentence

of stones so exactly puzzled not a blade of grass
could pass between: not a feather, not an eyelash. Not

the disk of a day moon; not the elbow of a shadow
razed from its house of desert sun, the thorned limb

scaled with insects clustered like a broken head
of wheat, the gleaner's fingers pursed to demonstrate

yield—not the mosquito slapped sipping
at the tail-thump of his wrist, but the clotted grains,

his transfigured palm rouged with the surfacing
opacity of cardinal nectar by which I mean

these girls' own burst bodies he holds
out, yes, for us.

Still Life with Damnosa Hereditas and Dark Constellations: USS *Arizona* and Llullaillaco Maiden

Undersea, the body
will arboresce, limbs branching to digits clarified

by dissolve—the mace-head of a sea urchin
jolting its spines from the emptied brainpan

like a light bulb's haloed rays sketched to signify
epiphany, what punctuated my father's life over bodies

of water. Night shift astern, that wake's mesmerizing
phosphorescent churn detonated a tiny star

in his brain, anchoring his entire life to one
unanswerable question. The woodiest tissue

spurs a bloom; from January nights, Christmas trees
keep rising to bruise the shallows

of my neighborhood's lake—water flea to seed
shrimp to crayfish to shad, chaining up to the bass the trees

were plunged there for. Any wreck
will harbor its pearls. Any glacier glanced through the glass

roof of a centipede train whitens sky to the spine
of a wind-lapped palm frond, cloud-shot with mornings

imminent with rain.

§

Growing up as the foot of mountains meant breathing day
as one-half shadow, one-half sun. We called it speed

to swallow flight; to keep our parents' fire
from our hair, we breathed heat

in, rolling up the backseat windows
so the comet tails of their lit cigarette butts sparked

off the glass, arcing away with a spray of tiny stars
red as cinders my sister slipped me from the secret spoon

of her fingernail. Our father always drove deep
into the meat of night. Black hush of midnight, our first

cross-country trip; black band of the Tennessee snagged
with glittering fallout—city lights a mirror writing he read

as second vision: that one day he'd live
in the South, meaning he knew even then

he would leave us. Black trees, black vines spilling
across tarmac. The promise of disappearance,

the deepest breath.

§

Pacific waters, dark swarm of planes

on dawn radar misread
as *friendly*—

black dragon, the flare's
signaling arc, a falling star triggering

the falling to a steaming

wreckage of light. The Milky Way's spine—
bright embers the dark

constellations entwine, gods animated
by the skeletons of shadows: the Llama,

the Fox; the Serpent, the Toad.
Moon a fisted cave spider dangling

between Andean peaks, moon across

Pacific waters: if a face, unfeatured
as any father, soldiering on.

Moon fisted between antlered peaks.

Moon scattered across harbored sea.

Dark constellations, dark swarm
on dawn radar.

§

                    Of the sacrificed
Children of the Cold, two girls; of two, the Maiden

best preserved. Unlike Lightning Girl, struck straight
through the ice, the Maiden's heart still flush, spidered

with ruby ice. Ice a composition of lace
stitching her arms' tiny hairs. Ice

the skeleton of her last breath, five hundred years and still
held. Caverned above the caldera, in the body

of ice, hers curled inward, the way the human
always will, faced with fire, laced with ice, beneath

the gods—dark eyes studding the Milky Way,
unblinking.

§

With our parents, there was so little drama.
There was silence. Only his heavy snoring ratcheting up

late nights, from the couch, and new furniture, plastic-
cauled, over months appearing

in the garage. When the moving van
finally arrived, my mother still hadn't asked,

am I to go with you?

My sister made her do it, ask.

§

                    Despite night's looming
freeze, calls of new frogs, threaded by the pull

of near spring, rise from the flooded field.
Once, my father netted me a glistening fist

from snow melt and rain, all eyes and silver tails: a cluster
of tadpoles. The watch of days we measured then

by each body's swell, each tail
sucking in, until each had abandoned the clouded

water of home we'd scooped to brim
the terrarium flush to its island masted with a single

plastic palm. Once, he came home staggering, leaves stuck
in his sweater, his hair. Once, he would eat dinner glancing always

sideways at the sideboard mirror, checking the movement
of his jaws—was he chomping, was he

gaping, was that boy, that furtive, bird-boned body caught
in the crook of his throat again

crowning, that overalled, shoeless boy he'd been
he'd so carefully caverned away behind his white

dress shirt, breast shadowed by the pocket Constitution
he always carried. He was looking to see

how he would be seen
by someone. My mother never asked

their names.

§

Dark meat around the bone-light of stars: *dark
constellations*, animate gods, open mouth of a hunger

a single girl never could fill.

§

To impregnate with spices;
to preserve from decay, by other means, as by cold.
To preserve from oblivion;

to keep in sweet and honored remembrance.
To steep.

Underground, his body floats his chosen
cargo of poison. Lightning girl, my mother
preferred ash. A wall faced with marble. *Remember*
as a word for *star*. A sky sometimes

to visit. The air that afternoon was numbing; no,
numb. A pocket Constitution I remember his student dropped
into the grave. A Navy bugler played Taps, music he'd loved
nights on watch.

§

In a museum absent of signage, the viewer can't miss
the missing, the single plucked strand unbraided

to revelation, each particular the girl
was fed the months before sacrifice, how she took it

all in, maize and coca, leaves balled to the green
wings her teeth still clench

in the X-ray. Outside, the signage of protest is over
her displacement, glacial chamber

to glass cube. Not over what placed her
in the ice to begin with. No flash

allowed, the eye must widen
against the dim: each panel a staircase

of eyes, such *exposure*, what downed her
degree by degree to this

precise stall.

§

Placed *in ordinary* first then struck
from the roster of ships—but he was not
on the *Arizona*, his only passed safely
over the wreckage to open
sea, epiphanic night—*why do men keep choosing*
what they despise, his question

about war a scene to revisit
in the memoir he left us
while my mother managed only
a single diary entry before abandoning
herself for the white-out
of blank pages. Witness

without word, word
without witness: each a lesser
than music, lesser than the hand's
embodied line, loop, dot,
cross.

§

What the membered body maps: not surface

but braid; not the blue sea water now shadowed by memorial
bridging the wreck; not the Convict Tangs

and Butterfly fish nudging fluttering fingers
of corals as they nozzle through a doorway on a deck

studded with mooring bitts like keys
on a flute; not the day's bloom, break

down, bloom of an hour's black ribbon
of oil, its scribbled leak like reel to reel tape

unscrolling, triggering devolution, amoeba to angel
wing to psychedelic paisley

wash, like surfacing shreds of blacklight posters
that papered my sister's basement

bedroom, but detritus mat and colonial
feather-duster worms, *biofouling* of the wreck equally composed

of the living and the dead, voices gone to iridescence
and salt as the field of ice creeps forward to close

the liquid eye, over what,
cold-blooded, has already stilled

beneath its lid.

§

Girl in the glass, to be visible
is to be food for the gods.

Boy in the mirror, any fabricated thing
held above the body patches the light
it meant to flag.

Memory cools toward infinite viscosity
which isn't true freezing.

Ice is what we make of the stars.

Still Life with Zodiac Boat and Glacier Lagoon

A bowl
of white
light, spiked
meringue peaks
debris-veined—
black ash
and graveled till,
blue-milk fins
calving
into melt;
too much to stay
against, one's
own weight borne
by speed, by wind
not weather
but the fast-
forward of a century
on fire
bulled forth
by my own eyes'
burning
toward sheered
sapphire, by
the pull cord's
raveling wick
with which I lit
this engine, this small
blind body
of need.

Third Cabinet

Still, with Judas Goats

Project Isabela, Galápagos

Selection began the terror: how I loved
my new necklace, His glittering noosed ear
always upon me. When He came first
from the sky, when He slipped

the hood over my horns, stood me
onto my shoulders, I felt a sting,
a clip, a brightness distancing
my body. As what had quickened in me

stilled in His hands, I knew He couldn't bear
to share me. Shot with the needle
dripping unending desire of others
for me, didn't I dutifully draw

my kind from their caves, making again
our little society? Forgive me, those days I almost
forgot Him. When the five-bladed sky
powered its seraphimed shadow

upon us, how we ran, I
with them—the ones who'd mounted
me, the little ones racing still
for their mothers' teats—how they dropped

to their knees, their legs snapped
broomsticks, leaves still spun from the glossy
corners of their mouths, their fur
glistening with rain-sleek roses, lipsticked kisses

blown from their bodies. But wasn't I
the beloved, the one left, taken again
under His wing, until it all again
began? How many times this occurred

is beyond my measure. Finally, I could gather
only those like me, the startled girls,
each of us taken in to believe we were
The One. We knew each other

by our war-slicked eyes, the echo
of our sutured, future-emptied bodies,
how we each wore the charm of His listening
around our neck. And no more

did the sky empty upon us, no more
did He come for us; the grass grew lush
under our few hooves, for we did not
increase, and the great ones who had long

withered inside their domed shells
began again to move among us.
The ones we now knew all
had been done for, though we were left

freely to eat what we would, what would have fed
so many lost we'd led. O God
in the Whirling Machine, didn't we well
bring your weather down?

Now we bow our heads only
to the recovering green.

Still Life with Wisteria Syndrome and Marula

Why, near sunset, such
humming to the trees? The eye
a blur of bees veering these lavender

pendulums—clusters half grape, half
orchid, declining vines, bicep-thick, spiraling
the slash pine. No wintered leaves

interred, the forest floor desert-bare
as the skirt of the marula autumned across
hemispheres and decades, where boys

steered skeletal cars fashioned from wire,
bits gathered first from fence trash to toy
nuts not from the untouched heart

of fallen fruits but from bone-clean stones
passed wholly through goats browsing still
the near thorns. As if defusing

tiny bombs, knuckle by knuckle: so it seemed,
looking on. *Once* is a tangle of intestines
dished as *serobe*, meat's bite a stain of sour

grass on the tongue; *once*, such fruit, the sun
downing, a brightness to the shifting
channel of flight: moths at the flowers

now, the powdery whirring of wings
shadowing what's left beneath the fading
firework-filaments of needles. *Do you*

remember, meaning *can something fallen*
still be eaten? Passed through the guts
of world, what drew her to the hair

trigger of a vine's arms splintered beyond
flowering to mouth those seeds not deadly
enough? Her arms, cocooned by no lasting

stillness, folding beneath her, but earth's near bare
horizon, sky a lit wing purpling with dusk, tongue
peppered with what couldn't be taken

and saved: O darkening she lay
in wanting, far side of no moon she'd set
even one more night sky by.

Still Life with Phantom Crane Fly and Vanity Mirror

Absent the light-speckled thicket camouflage is lost
her zebraed legs   triple-jointed quills like folding

seeing-eye canes half-ratcheted   splayed
into place   a bruised lilt as she lurches

her stilled wings the veined gauze
of obsolescence riding the fan's current

that's caught her   a cottonwood's
parachuting seed   an image

of home you keep
dreaming as a mortgage you'd signed

and somehow forgotten   the house
rotting without you   and you living

basement by basement   what you'd witnessed
in swamped forest air   spectacle's creature

a dozen unspooling legs just a tangled
mating   your bed long made

beneath bare-bulbed earth   shelved one-
eighty-proof rum   the Ford you'd street-raced

through neighborhoods kept
taking you nowhere and one night

into a ditch   the dealer you idolized the one
you let drive   you passed out proving

you were your father's daughter and could
take it   his name was Trip   his name

wasn't Trip he was famous for the huge
falling-down house he'd kept

a half-dozen runaways at to sell
for him   including your friend Troy

in the backseat   how nostalgic they were
for that lost house   you kept for two years

in a nightstand drawer the rolled socks he left
that night in your car   as if you could remember him

unpeeling them   maybe they're still there the way
heroin killed Troy but not

for decades   the way your ghosted jaw would ache
when you'd wake unable to voice

the difference between seedpod
and wing   the thready body

both labyrinth and a taut
unspooling   legs hollow   breathing

a diffusion   batting the silvered surface the slivered
room   that expansive mirage

sealed there   the glass you slip over her
you cup your hand there   fling her

out the window   some other breeze
to catch her   one you didn't

snap on by a switch igniting
the wall   his name was Jerome   *I*

was an acid trail in a set
of fitting room mirrors

dissolving to *you*   vacancy chain
in reverse   you learned to be by being

least   most distant   the O
so gullible one batting a fractured

room of glass   you let her go   rather
I made her gone

Still, with Trip

Trick isn't in wining,
dining: hit,

miss. Trick is picking
with skill, gilding

this girl driving
blind; priming girl-bits

with quick highs: spliff,
gin; brimming

in blitz—it isn't will
inviting will, it's

jiving, it's timing
stripping this listing

thing: prizing thighs,
pinning wrists, ribs,

lips, with hips, prick,
imprinting *I*: minting

in child, Bitch.
This skirt-hiking

giving-in isn't limb
stitching limb, skin

spicing skin: it's
circling, it's wing-

clipping, divining chinks I
fist in. It's winning.

This pitch, this flinch—
writhing is icing, I drink it

in. Slick Wiz I, I'm chill,
I'm with it—Christ, I'm

striking it rich. Skill,
wit, this stiff hilt I

swing: I'm His
gift. If light's listing ship

is sinking, if civil
twilight, virgin

night, is tiding in,
it isn't I: girls

spirit sin. Which split,
drifting girl's filth

will I witch this night?
Miss Shrinking Girl, Miss

Whining Girl, Miss Victim,
Miss Pills / Slit-Wrist Girl:

Miss Scribbling Girl, sling it
shrill, hiss with infin-

iting might. Dish it.
I'm thick brick. Sick strict

in bridling, I'm whipping
birch limbs, I'm disciplining

lightning. Girl, bring it.
Biding, I bind. I'm

whistling, I'm
spiking it in. High sign.

Kiss kiss. Dig it: I'm still
riding high.

Still Life with Lightning Whelk and Columbarium

Living the dark
days of the future, the architect angled
    for sky—a mocked-
up chapel, a spire's
    prismed spike: all those tiny
severed rooms. Spring again's a wash
    of egg casings, like chains of blonde seaweed
tangled ashore: here a serifed spine, there
a sundered arm. Tattered
    and toothy, all those braceleted
blown pods, and the one
    still shrouded—an infant stilled

in its caul. A certain economy
    to the dead, this minimal
exertion to memory: dovecote
    or necropolis, the face is a winged
    veil, a bell cave secreting
its cinerary urn, a blocked-letter name
    stick-crossing the grained
facade like an urchin's
    snapped spines, like shell fragments
so aligned in sand as to appear
    treasure, an outsized

singularity. Distinctly
    lightning, the sinistral shell; any
whelk's, the barbed
marble crest, the nipple
    of ossified air topping the false
nautilus swirl any cathedral's spiraling
    staircase would have the eye
    look up to through the marred heart
of spin. To sketch
    the shadowed steps, sun-spiked lashes

halo the scepter, the shell's mace
     and drill, its mute

nacre-less ribs. The wall
filling, all those put-out pearls
     of window light; or vessels
post storm, low tide's *finds* late sun
glisters, rending curtains
     of ash to fire that perfect
gathering: the whole drowned world
salted over, sparking.

Fourth Cabinet

Still, with the Coming Extinction of the Southern African Donkey

Where your ridge of winter-thinned limbs
hung our shoulders vulture-heavy

with mist; where floods thrust your glassed sky
up to the knotted knees

of fence posts, anthills erupting
so hock to fetlock we ran with the trailed mouth

of fire; where thorns' shadow-casings alone
blackened the sand, the ground we knew

most, who all our lives balanced the shift
of shatter beneath our hooves—didn't

we bear it, all of it, never kicking free
of your hobbles? Didn't we do your bidding, even

in chains? And when, from beyond
the sea's bounds, others came, didn't we trust

their careful calculations were born solely
of salt, of distance mated with flawed

faith, what lay beyond our understanding not
the small money that swayed you, not the cracked

bullet-ridden sky, nor those that struck
home, our voiced bones left cradling a fever beyond

our bridling, but you, calming us
into the thorn-bush kraal we'd known only

as night's rest, how we, just the youngest among us
softly braying, again followed the leathered whip

of your hand. How we lay dazed
and freighted, as one by one they sawed us free

of what they coveted, trucking away
our skin, that thin blurred line all that had held us to

and from you, who are left a strange
silence, our ragged

leavings—collateral, our meat, was it sweet
in your mouths we'd so long

filled, yoked one to one to the teeth
of the plow, your world growing behind us,

furrowed, expectant? Didn't we crop
the bone grass only, leaving sorghum, maize,

the miracle of desert melon sprouting
from our forward ache before we learned to curse

our prayer: May our absence grow wild
all of your days, shrouding

your unstrung carts, your water tanks
throat-open to harvest rain

from thin air; may your choked fields sing
only hunger's growl, the drummed hollow we so long

had stomached, docile as we were,
then, before we dared be

the ghosts that now, into the flaming
plumes of dust, always

will bear you.

Still Life with January

Measure the heart by obsession, and the tablets click
in their plastic sheath like a shaker

of salt, crystals fused to small stones
absent the rice grains that would have held

back the weeping as attendant to southern air
as water falling through rock we traced

to a mint-green pool's back-story grotto sculpted
to snowy scallops, pale husks tossed

entirely of spray. Ice, you'd say, is a giving
up of energy; to crystal is to displace

a mineral dissolve best crossed by trusting the rawest,
unslicked rocks topping that afternoon's

half-frozen falls before your shift pieced with the passing
of prescription papers fingerprinted and spored

with viruses' spiny stars, night a soup of swamp-lunged children
and a man drunk to the bone who, having stitched

his own ripped tongue with fishing line, leans
your counter to ask, *this will be awright,*

right?; night-rollers who troll your store's fluorescent aisles
for Sudafed and watch batteries, matches and fingernail

polish remover, passing the wandering afflicted
shaking off voices amplified by hollow, the silvered foil hat

of wakefulness; the simpático adding the zeroes
of their own hand to tens on scrips for Oxy you refuse

to fill, thus troubling their ascent to that extended
blessing—O pills to parachute, O to dive that high

my own once-husband sought in a free-based implosion
to a sinkhole of blacked foil and glass pipes and stolen

checks, my mother's signature steadied in his adrenaline-
laced hand, shattered car-window glass glistening our alley's

graveled snow, crook of a missing tire iron
ghosting me still. Glitter beyond the body's breadth, cliffs

whiskered with icicles, automatic glass doors folding
the drone of 3 a.m. for the man in black-face and hoodie

who'd jump your counter, knife in hand, for what he would first
have you live for—to open the narc safe, portal

to that sustained sustenance, O perpetual
plunge. What persists is less

the print he'd left in his own shoe polish-smeared face
than his fingertips' stain, the drop of soiled sweat tracing

his cheek's descent like the bead of melt already grooving that day's
translucent heart, a hollowed pinprick sunlit to a mercury globe

tonguing its way down the shelved stone wall bracketed
with daggered racks of moony glass, gravity-pooling to the path

deeply sheeted to shadowboxes of pine needle and fern
and sweetgum leaf, glazed skin delicately grained and insect-whorled

as the human palm, as yours I worried
that afternoon into mine. In review, the cameras

stagger events: the knife ratcheting toward your chest skips
to the man's spectacular crashing the thickly paned

door, but *when*, not *where*, is the heart
of dissolve; each body of glass tunes to its own

one-note shatter, your face held there
in fracture, in stone a spring day's warming can vanish—stalactites

that for now narrow, swell, narrow, clocking the hours' shift
freeze to melt to freeze along the banded fault lines

of history where a sweetgum rises from the thinnest outcrop
rooted with icicles like weighted ropes pulled taut

from a bridge, time progressing in freefall as one camera skips
to the next, to the man stumbling into the night, the dropped knife

skittering the iced pavement and in that blackened air, what I've held
on for—gauze of your glittering breath, O

collateral grace.

Still, with I

I

Girl inscribing in night
lightning's sizzling trill,

whittling in pitch this bright
wiring, its divining stick's split

kindling his witching wick, his
birdish ribs, wish's thin fit;

girl, this wild which births limb
twining limb will still spirit

chill, flirt's flit stilling

II

in flint. Girl mimicking

his wit's gimmick, chiming
his insist—his *is*, his *isn't*—kinking

his whip, kinging him
with rings, with *in thick,*

in thin, with pink icing's
gilding scrim: in blinks, hitch

is pinch, listing in wind
his riffing wrists silk. Instinct's

first high diminishing

III

in fifths. Girl skirting lightning

shrinking thin, thirst circling
his brim, *I* isn't *I*

if middling in him.
If hindsight is insight

biding its timing, *might*
is might. Girl still rinsing

in light, this spring's
still high: Girl, sink.

Swim.

Still Life with Caribbean Reef Squid (*Sepioteuthis sepioidea*)

What swam back from the doe-damp eye—
your own goggled face, unfinished
as the goby's you treaded sea against

the surf's surging to witness emerge
from its brain-coral cave, that fogged, head-
on perspective rendering it simple

beyond its being: a gas-masked gesture drawing
crosshatched to shadows. As against high-cotton
rag paper, stroke by stroke you remember

a man who sketched you as you slept, packing
on charcoal until it approximated
the darkness the face meant to rise

against. You saw it before you knew
its name, knowing only the creature
had seen you, knowing this only by its quick

disappearance. But the squid
do not startle. Fins rippling, sleek bodies gleaming
liquid as wax sprung from the head

cavity of a sperm whale sparked to specter
the flame it would wick to only when the knives
were docked, their arms extend, mimicking

sargassum weed: hovering, though you know
what's coming, still it surprises, how sudden
the unfurling, the arms flash-flowering to star

anemone, how fierce their drilling the dark
pockets for what harbored in the hope
refuge might lie in a bed

of hard corals. How you trailed this ravenous
unfolding, shadowing their trolling
the fringe reef—iridescent, crushed-pearl mounds

studded with fan corals lavender and lime, royal
purple, waved from stiff wrists of holdfasts
by leeward's muted, moon-driven surf. Dusky

anchovy. Hardhead silversides. Shrimp, dwarf
herring: all things soft, devoured. All things armored,
discarded: head-ribs-vertebral column a single

unsheathing. To walk on water is to miss
this world by half: this, immersion
taught you. No alarm's gold brightening, no brick

red of retreat. No diversion of ink clouding their swerve
into distance. Like sequins cast in organza
veils, a spray of sinkers woven to fishing nets'

translucence, they signed each to each
in shimmering chromatics you could read only
as radiance, diminishment

propelling you on. Whether hours or minutes,
you could not say. You followed. Then, led
to the coral's fossil-strewn shore, the shell

of you returned.

Still Life with Bloodroot (*Sanguinaria canadensis*)

Brain-veined, cabbaged
around a single bud, in barest canopy
your one, winged leaf unfurls
to a lemon crown of anthers, to ghost-white petals' quick
thinning to translucence, to capsule
unzipping its pod of pursed seeds nut-brown, glossy
as tiger eye, elaiosomes' umbilical froth
coiling each globed bead—the dormant future figured
as apple, and worm, though your whole
is generative: even these filmy members
winnow ants—copper baubles spider-wired
to filigree—feed their young, leaving the seed to sprout
from nest debris. There are those who thrive
in margins, who survive the wild
shrinking: coyote, raccoon, dandelion; fire ants
overrunning forest and field, who take the bait but
destroy the seed. Outsiders, how can we help
but hunger? Bloodroot, you unscroll
to the staggered world of fence posts
no new flowers. Your given name a study in slicing
a clotted root to bleed, this world so beautiful
we could eat you whole: Blood Root,
Red Root, Tetterwort, Sweet Slumber—nest
I call you by, scouting your woods;
whether as winnow- or fire- I come
to you, what begins each spring
one more vanishing.

Still Life with Evolution: *Amblyrhynchus cristatus* (Marine Iguana), Fernandina, Galápagos

Never was a dry eye into the continent; never a land bridge, but a raft
of storm trash, and twisted into the trees' risen roots, woven
into wreaths of floating mangrove, the long-snouted ancestor
that captain's companion Darwin stumbled into their
beginning from. That human eyes, like a bird's, can mirror
the viewer, can hold her as a tiny floating thing, is a condition,
not the accomplishment, of empathy. Which is weightless
as these skeletons a wind skitters, wedging to crooks
between rocks the curved spines, vertebrae puzzled knuckle
to knuckle—some like antique-ivory combs, the teeth
snapped off; some still rayed with ribs like the straws
of lost-wax castings, splayed to a galley's oars, stalled
as the day the sea glassed and the Spanish bishop's sails
unspooled, drawing him near enough to be appalled
less by their hundreds' braiding to a mass ropy
as the pāhoehoe bones bearing them, than by their likeness,
that face isolation's million generations had blunted

so near his own. Scaled to minute pyramids, Brutalist
castles, the forehead is distance ranged as caldera-capped peaks.
A lace skull cap of sneezed salt. Because what sustains, too long
held, poisons, and what they must eat swells so richly
with it, the moats lacing the scales' pinnacled plates pulse
neon-green with the crystalline desiccation of seaweed
the largest will dive for, straight into the frigid surf
dropping them, degree by degree, towards muscles' freeze
and no more rising. So tuned to what haloes, half their work
is warming, spreadeagled, bean-bag heavy against a shelf
of black rock all glass and pocketed air where flat
on my stomach I lay to meet the cabbed gembones
of one's eyes. So close, my breath—were this some
northern winter—might have gloved him. Yet no flinch,
no turn. To be held in such trust is to be at once
invisible and so deeply seen that no reflection mars
the eye, unblinking: though in truth, this grace they'll grant

anything not hawk, their one predator on this still
cat-free island. Nothing here yet feral. Nothing yet slipping
into burrows, sliding their leathery eggs down throats
fluent as five centuries of naming weighting their backs
like the hawk, descending, who could not both fight
and lift the heaviest, who must press his prey against
the noon-warmed stone until it stills. Imps of Darkness.
Hideous Creatures. Cooking the body in its own skin,
not to death but paralysis, flipping it, ripping into the soft
belly to begin. Tiny T-Rex. Mini Godzilla. Ancient Days Come
Once More to Earth. The mockingbird's alert call the one
sound true: a one-noted, deep-throated strobe meaning *hawk*
they've learned to distinguish from the bird's
trilling song. To survive a lean year, the seaweed's
dying down, they'll digest their own bones: the pattern

was predictable; a year's warmed water to be followed
by many more, cooling. Those with the deepest hunger,
who could not hold out even a single season: those skeletons
are theirs, lacing the black boulders, devolving
toward air. *Good bones,* we say of a house worth saving.
Good bones. Such stiff grace, such sinuous
articulation, the long tails propelling them
through the rough current, the limbs, their outsized
claws, held tight and still against the rigid torso,
the dorsal crest's ash-green spines a fringed fin
arcing the surface it parts. The architecture of the body
is ark and cage, and home is another island's harbor
where a grounded hull, listing starboard, ribbons out oil
silking to an iridescent skin. Beauty isn't beauty, isn't
truth, what cannot be scooped in nets,
what cannot be scrubbed from the chosen few plucked
from blackened beaches: the temperature scaling beyond

the seaweed's bearing. Unchained offshore, my ship
purrs. I was never harmless, though I lay as still
as a breathing body might. Cooling by facing head-on
the heat, the colony orients entire towards the noon sun,
their silence punctuated, as with coughs in a darkening
theater, by this sibilance, expelling the one poison
they'd been gifted a world of time to grow to. Never will be
a land bridge. *Never* is a dry eye into every continent.
In my breath, the flood and the fire
rising. And beyond, the sound of a great gathering,
listening.